God Said To Me

Your Job Is To

Love

By
Frank J. Donohue

Not-Y, Virginia Beach

Copyright Notice

Dedication

I dedicate this to book Francis John, Jared
Joseph and to all lovers and non-lovers.

Contents

Introduction

John, a remarkable individual, embodied not only a big and tall physical presence but also a heart overflowing with kindness and warmth. His superlative niceness and friendly nature drew people towards him, making him a beloved companion to walk alongside. I have many fond memories of walking and laughing with pilot friend John. His infectious laughter, filled with joy and mirth, seemed to have no end, brightening the lives of those fortunate enough to share in his company.

John had embarked on a remarkable career as a pilot, traversing the skies and exploring the vastness of the world. For many years, he piloted planes across different continents, allowing him to witness firsthand the captivating beauty of diverse countries and cultures. The intricacies of flight, the art of maneuvering through the heavens, held a profound fascination for him. The sense of freedom that enveloped him as he soared through the skies was a sensation he cherished, and it shaped his perspective on life.

John's experiences as a pilot undoubtedly contributed to his understanding of the interconnectedness of humanity. He had the privilege of witnessing the world from a unique vantage point, soaring above borders and realizing the inherent similarities that unite people across different nations. He recognized that we are all interconnected in this vast tapestry of life.

But one day in September, while John was soaring over the vast expanse of the ocean, he had an experience that shook him to his core. As he piloted the aircraft, a supernatural and awe-inspiring feeling enveloped him, and suddenly, he heard a voice resounding within him—a voice that he instinctively recognized as the unmistakable voice of God.

Frank, who had been captivated by John's story, couldn't help but feel a sense of astonishment as he listened to the revelation.

This profound encounter became the defining moment that compelled Frank to pen this book, driven by the urgency to share John's transformative journey.

In December, with a heart brimming with vulnerability and openness, John confided in Frank, disclosing the remarkable truth. "Frank," John revealed, "God appeared to me in a voice that reverberated through my being, and He spoke these words to me: 'Your job is to love.'"

Frank himself was taken aback by this revelation, unable to fathom the magnitude of what John had experienced. The notion of God directly addressing John, entrusting him with such a profound purpose, left Frank in awe. "Your job is to love," the voice had declared, a statement that reverberated within John's being, challenging him to comprehend its profound implications.

Overwhelmed by the weight of this extraordinary encounter, John found himself in a state of stunned disbelief. Never before had he encountered anything of this nature, and the sheer reality of God speaking directly to him seemed almost too incredible to fathom. "Your job is to love," the voice reiterated, its clarity and strength leaving an indelible impression upon John's soul. Perplexed, he sought to comprehend the meaning behind these words, prompting him to ask, and "What do you mean?" The voice responded, unwavering and resolute, "Your job is to love."

John thought about what the voice had said for a long time. He tried to process what he had just heard. But as he thought about it more, he realized that this message was one that he had been searching for his entire life.

For years, John had been searching for meaning and purpose in his life. He had flown planes all over the world, but he had always felt like something was missing. Now, with this message from God, he realized that he had been searching in the wrong place all along.

As he continued to fly, John began to think more deeply about what it meant to love. He realized that loving others was about more than just being kind or polite. It was about truly caring for others and showing them compassion, even in the face of difficulty or adversity.

John loved his flying and was very good at it. He was always careful to follow safety procedures and to take care of his health.

About a month after his spiritual encounter with God, John was flying a plane when he noticed the skin abrasion on his buttocks still did not go away. He initially didn't think much of it but on this particular day it bothered him. John mentioned it to a pilot doctor friend, who recommended he see a dermatologist.

John went to the doctor, who diagnosed him with necrotizing fasciitis. Necrotizing fasciitis is a rare but serious bacterial infection that can quickly spread through the body. It can cause death if it is not treated promptly. The doctor told John that he needed to be hospitalized. He was given antibiotics and surgery to remove the infected tissue. A few days later, John started to feel sick. He had a fever, chills, and a headache. He also had a lot of pain in his buttocks.

Here are some additional details about necrotizing fasciitis:

- Necrotizing fasciitis is caused by a group of bacteria that live in the environment.

These bacteria can enter the body through a break in the skin, such as a cut or a burn.

- Necrotizing fasciitis can spread quickly through the body. It can cause death within hours if it is not treated promptly.

- The symptoms of necrotizing fasciitis include:

  - Fever

  - Chills

  - Headache

  - Pain in the affected area

  - Redness, swelling, and warmth in the affected area

  - Blisters on the skin

  - Skin that feels hard or feels like it is "giving way"

If you think you might have necrotizing fasciitis, it is important to see a doctor right away. Early diagnosis and treatment are essential for a good outcome.

John entered into a coma, a deep state of unconsciousness where a person is unable to respond to stimuli.

Life After Death experiences have been reported since the dawn of time. Near-death experiences (NDEs) have been reported by individuals who have come close to death, and in some cases, were clinically dead. NDEs often involve a variety of spiritual and life-altering experiences.

These individuals often report feeling a sense of peace, seeing a bright light, and feeling a sense of detachment from their physical body. Some also report having an out-of-body experience where they feel like they are hovering above their physical body. They often report seeing a realm of existence that exists beyond this physical world, and some even report meeting deceased relatives. Those who have had life after death experiences also report spiritual encounters with the afterlife. These encounters often involve sensing a presence or feeling a connection to a higher power or a realm of existence that exists beyond this physical world. Some individuals have reported communicating with deceased relatives or even God.

These spiritual encounters are often described as peaceful, comforting, and enlightening. While the details of each NDE vary, they often involve an individual's return to earth, usually with a heightened sense of love and appreciation for life. Returning to earth after a near-death experience is often described as a powerful, life-changing event.

Those who have experienced an NDE often report feeling an overwhelming sense of love and acceptance, and a deeper appreciation for the beauty of life and its fragility. They describe a newfound understanding of their purpose and place in the world, and a newfound respect for the interconnectedness of all things. Returning to earth after a near-death experience can also bring with it a newfound understanding of the power of love. Those who have experienced an NDE often report feeling an even greater capacity for love, both for themselves and for others. They describe a newfound sense of empathy, compassion, and understanding, and a greater openness to giving and receiving love. Manny who has experienced NDE believed the reason they were returned to planet Earth, and receive a second chance of life, was to learn to love more and to increase their capacity to give and receive love. Manny was convinced that the reason they were returned to planet Earth was to fulfill a fundamental purpose of their existence: to love and be loved.

This divine communication from God became the catalyst that set John's life on an extraordinary trajectory, compelling him to embark on a journey of love and selflessness. The profound impact of this revelation would shape the course of his life and serve as the guiding principle that propelled him to inspire others through his acts of kindness and generosity.

1

The Calling: When God Speaks

Why am I here … what is my purpose?

As human beings, we are constantly searching for meaning and purpose in our lives. We ask ourselves, "Why am I here?" and "What is my purpose?" For many people, the answer to these questions comes from their faith and their belief in God. In some cases, people feel that God has called them to a specific mission or purpose, and this is what we refer to as a "calling."

When we speak of a "calling," it is not just any ordinary job or career that we choose. It is something that we believe we are meant to do, that we are uniquely qualified for, and that we feel compelled to pursue. A calling is not just a job; it is a higher purpose, a divine mission that we believe we are called to fulfill.

In this chapter, we will explore the idea of a calling and how it relates to our relationship with God. We will look at the different ways that people experience a calling, and what it means to answer that call. We will also explore some of the challenges that come with answering a calling, and how we can stay true to our mission even in the face of adversity.

The concept of a calling is not a new one. Throughout history, people have felt called to various missions and purposes, from prophets and apostles to activists and humanitarian workers. The Bible is filled with stories of people who were called by God to fulfill a specific purpose. One such example is the prophet Isaiah, who received a vision from God in which he was called to speak to the people of Israel and urge them to repent.

In modern times, people continue to feel a calling from God. Some people are called to become pastors or missionaries, while others are called to work in social justice or humanitarian causes. Whatever the calling may be it is something that is deeply personal and often life-changing.

One of the most common ways that people experience a calling is through prayer and meditation. Many people report feeling a sense of clarity and direction during their quiet times with God. Others may have a sudden realization or moment of clarity that they feel is a message from God. Still, others may feel a calling through a dream or vision.

However, not everyone experiences a calling in the same way. Some people may have a more gradual realization that they are meant to do something specific, while others may feel an intense urgency to act immediately. It is important to remember that there is no one right way to experience a calling. The important thing is to listen to the still, small voice of God and be open to what He is calling us to do.

Once we have received a calling, the next step is to answer it. This can be a challenging process, as answering a calling often requires sacrifice and stepping outside of our comfort zones. We may have to give up certain things in order to pursue our mission, such as a steady job or a comfortable lifestyle. We may also face opposition or criticism from others who do not understand our calling.

Despite these challenges, answering a calling can be one of the most rewarding experiences of our lives. When we are doing what we were created to do, we feel a sense of fulfillment and purpose that cannot be found in any other way. We are living out our true identity and making a positive impact on the world around us.

In conclusion, a calling is something that many people experience at some point in their lives. It is a higher purpose, a divine mission that we feel compelled to pursue. When we listen to the voice of God and answer our calling, we can find meaning, purpose, and fulfillment in our lives. However, answering a calling is not always easy, and we may face challenges along the way. It is important to stay true to our mission and trust in God.

2

Love as a Divine Mission

Love is at the heart of many religions.

Love is a central theme in many religions
and spiritual practices. It is often referred to
as a divine force that connects us to one
another and to God. In this chapter, we will
explore the concept of love as a divine
mission, and how it relates to our
relationship with God and our purpose in
life.

Love is often described as a feeling,
but it is also an action. It is something that
we do, rather than just something that we
feel. Love is the act of putting others before
ourselves, of showing kindness, compassion,
and generosity. Love is not just about
romantic relationships or family
connections; it is something that we can

extend to all people, regardless of their background or beliefs.

In many religions, love is seen as a central tenet. For example, in Christianity, Jesus taught that the greatest commandment was to love God with all your heart, soul, and mind, and to love your neighbor as yourself. Similarly, in Islam, the Prophet Muhammad taught that love and compassion were essential to following God's will. In Buddhism, love and compassion are seen as the key to achieving enlightenment and ending suffering.

Love is not just a concept in religion, but it is also a scientific reality. Studies have shown that people who experience love and connection with others are happier, healthier, and live longer than those who do not. Love is also an essential component of human development, particularly in the early years of life. Babies who receive love and attention from their caregivers are more likely to grow up to be well-adjusted adults.

When we view love as a divine mission, it takes on a greater significance. We begin to see our relationships with others as part of a larger purpose, a mission that we are called to fulfill. Our mission is not just to love those who are easy to love, but to extend love to all people, even those who may be difficult or different from us.

Loving others can also be a way of expressing our love for God. When we show kindness, compassion, and generosity to others, we are reflecting God's love back into the world. We become agents of love, spreading positivity and joy wherever we go.

However, loving others is not always easy. We may encounter people who are difficult to love, or situations that challenge our ability to show kindness and compassion. It is in these moments that our love becomes a true mission. We must make a conscious effort to extend love even when it is difficult, to put aside our own needs and desires in order to serve others.

One of the most powerful ways to express love as a divine mission is through acts of service. Serving others is a way of demonstrating our love and commitment to them, and it is a practical way of making a positive impact on the world. Service can take many forms, from volunteering at a local charity to donating money or resources to those in need.

However, love as a divine mission is not just about doing good for others; it is also about transforming ourselves. When we make a conscious effort to love others, we become more compassionate, empathetic, and understanding. We begin to see the world in a different light, one that is characterized by love and kindness rather than fear and hostility.

In conclusion, love is a central theme in many religions and spiritual practices. When we view love as a divine mission, it takes on a greater significance. Our mission is not just to love those who are easy to love, but to extend love to all people, even those who may be difficult or different from us. Loving others can also be a way of expressing our love for God and making a positive impact on the world. By making a conscious effort to love others, we can transform ourselves and the world around us.

3

What is Love? Understanding God's Definition

Love is a feeling and an action.

Love is a complex concept that has been explored by philosophers, scientists, and theologians for centuries. At its core, love is an emotional state that is often associated with affection, warmth, and caring. But what is love from a spiritual perspective? In this chapter, we will explore the definition of love according to God and how it differs from the secular definition.

God's definition of love is rooted in the idea of selflessness. Love is not just a feeling, but it is an action that is motivated by a desire to put others before us. Love, according to God, is a sacrificial act of service and kindness that seeks the good of others above our own.

The Bible is full of examples of love in action. One of the most well-known is the story of Jesus Christ, who sacrificed his life for the redemption of humanity. In John 15:13, Jesus says, "Greater love has no one than this, that someone lay down his life for his friends." This act of selfless love is the ultimate example of what love should look like according to God.

God's definition of love is also characterized by forgiveness. Love is not just about doing good for others, but it is also about forgiving those who have wronged us. In Matthew 6:14-15, Jesus says, "For if you forgive others their trespasses, your heavenly Father will also forgive you, but if you do not forgive others their trespasses, neither will your Father forgive your trespasses." Forgiveness is a crucial component of love, as it allows us to move past hurt and resentment and towards healing and reconciliation.

Another aspect of God's definition of love is that it is not based on conditions or expectations. We are called to love others unconditionally, regardless of their behavior or circumstances. In 1 Corinthians 13:4-8, the apostle Paul describes love as patient, kind, not envious, not boastful, not arrogant, not rude, not selfish, not easily angered, and not keeping record of wrongs. These attributes are not contingent on the behavior of others, but are instead a reflection of the kind of love that God has for us.

God's definition of love is also characterized by its universality. Love is not just something that we extend to those who are close to us, but it is something that we can extend to all people, regardless of their background or beliefs. In Matthew 5:43-44, Jesus says, "You have heard that it was said, 'Love your neighbor and hate your enemy.' But I tell you, love your enemies and pray for those who persecute you." This command to love our enemies is a reminder that love is not limited by boundaries or circumstances.

From a secular perspective, love is often viewed as a feeling that is based on attraction or emotional connection. However, God's definition of love is much deeper and more profound. Love is an action that is motivated by a desire to serve others and put their needs before our own. It is characterized by forgiveness, universality, and an absence of conditions or expectations.

Understanding God's definition of love can be transformative in our relationships with others. When we view love as a selfless act of service, we are motivated to extend it to all people, regardless of their behavior or circumstances. When we embrace forgiveness as an essential component of love, we can move past hurt and resentment towards healing and reconciliation. And when we love unconditionally, we create an environment of kindness, compassion, and generosity that can change the world.

In conclusion, God's definition of love is different from the secular definition. Love is not just a feeling, but it is an action that is rooted in selflessness, forgiveness, and sacrifice.

4

The Power of Love: Changing Lives and Changing the World

Release your most powerful weapon - love.

Love has the power to change lives and change the world. It is a force that can transform hearts, heal wounds, and inspire greatness. Throughout history, we have seen examples of love's power in action, from the selfless sacrifice of Jesus Christ to the tireless work of activists and humanitarians around the globe. In this chapter, we will explore the transformative power of love and how it can change lives and change the world.

One of the most significant ways in which love can change lives is through personal transformation. When we experience love from others, it has the power to heal wounds and transform our perspective. It can help us to see others and ourselves in a new light, and it can motivate us to become better versions of ourselves. This transformation can be seen in the lives of countless individuals who have been touched by the love of family, friends, or even strangers.

Love can also change lives by breaking down barriers and building bridges between individuals and communities. When we extend love to others, we create a connection that transcends our differences and brings us together. This connection can be seen in the work of organizations that bring together people from different backgrounds and cultures to work towards a common goal.

One example of the power of love to break down barriers is the civil rights movement in the United States. Led by figures such as Martin Luther King Jr., the movement was fueled by a deep love for justice and equality. It brought together individuals from different races, religions, and backgrounds to fight for the rights of African Americans. Through their love and sacrifice, they were able to bring about significant social and political change.

Love can also change the world by inspiring acts of kindness and compassion. When we witness acts of love from others, it can inspire us to do the same. This ripple effect of love can create a chain reaction of kindness that can transform entire communities and even nations. This is evident in the work of humanitarian organizations that provide aid and support to those in need, often in the most challenging and dangerous circumstances.

One example of the power of love to inspire acts of kindness is the work of Mother Teresa. Known for her tireless work with the poor and sick, Mother Teresa's love and compassion inspired countless individuals around the world to serve others in need. Her example shows that one person's love and sacrifice can have a ripple effect that extends far beyond them.

Love can also change the world by challenging us to think beyond our own interests and ourselves. When we love others, we are motivated to seek their good above our own. This can inspire us to work towards a better world for all people, regardless of their background or circumstances. This motivation for the common good can be seen in the work of social and environmental activists who work tirelessly to create a more just and sustainable world.

One example of the power of love to inspire action for the common good is the environmental movement. Motivated by a deep love and respect for the earth and its creatures, environmental activists work to protect and preserve our planet for future generations. Their love for the earth inspires them to take action, from small acts of conservation to large-scale advocacy and policy change.

In conclusion, the power of love to change lives and change the world is undeniable. It has the power to transform hearts, break down barriers, inspire acts of kindness and compassion, and challenge us to work towards the common good. As individuals and communities, we have the opportunity to harness the transformative power of love to create a better world for future generations and ourselves.

5

The Challenges of Loving: Overcoming Fear, Anger, and Hate

Increase the strength of your inner willpower to love.

While the power of love is undeniable, it is not always easy to love. In a world filled with conflict, injustice, and pain, it can be challenging to extend love to others, especially those who have hurt us or those who are different from us. In this chapter, we will explore the challenges of loving and how we can overcome fear, anger, and hate to extend love to all people.

One of the primary challenges of loving is fear. Fear can manifest in many ways, from a fear of rejection to a fear of vulnerability. When we are afraid, we may struggle to open ourselves up to others and extend love. However, as we have seen in previous chapters, love requires vulnerability and openness. We cannot love if we are not willing to be vulnerable and open ourselves up to the possibility of hurt.

To overcome fear, we must cultivate courage. This means acknowledging our fears and choosing to act in spite of them. We must recognize that loving others requires risk and that the potential reward of deep and meaningful relationships is worth the risk. This courage can be cultivated through small acts of vulnerability and stepping out of our comfort zones.

Another challenge of loving is anger. Anger can arise when we feel hurt or wronged by others, and it can make it difficult to extend love. However, anger can also be a motivator for change. When we channel our anger towards positive action, we can create change in ourselves and in the world around us.

To overcome anger, we must learn to channel it in a positive way. This means recognizing when we are feeling angry and choosing to respond in a way that is productive and constructive. This can involve setting boundaries, having difficult conversations, or taking action to address injustice. When we use our anger as a motivator for positive change, we can transform it into a force for good.

Hate is perhaps the most significant challenge to loving. Hate can arise from fear and anger, but it is characterized by a dehumanization of others. When we hate, we see others as less than human and justify mistreating them. Hate can manifest in many ways, from racism and sexism to bigotry and intolerance.

To overcome hate, we must recognize the humanity in others. This means seeing them as individuals with their own stories, struggles, and dreams. We must cultivate empathy and seek to understand the experiences and perspectives of those who are different from us. This can involve challenging our own biases and assumptions and being open to learning from others.

We must also be willing to confront hate when we see it. This means speaking out against bigotry and intolerance, even when it is uncomfortable or unpopular. We must be willing to stand up for what is right, even when it is difficult.

In conclusion, the challenges of loving are significant, but they are not insurmountable. We can overcome fear, anger, and hate by cultivating courage, channeling our anger in a positive way, and recognizing the humanity in others. By doing so, we can extend love to all people, regardless of their background or circumstances. We can create a more just and compassionate world.

6

Loving Yourself: The Foundation of Loving Others

If you don't like what you see in the mirror, change it.

In the previous chapters, we have discussed the importance of love and the challenges that come with extending love to others. In this chapter, we will explore the often-overlooked aspect of loving oneself and how it is the foundation for loving others.

Loving oneself is often seen as selfish or egotistical, but this is a misconception. Self-love is not about prioritizing one's own needs above others, but rather recognizing that loving oneself is essential for loving others. When we love ourselves, we are better equipped to love others because we have a solid foundation of self-respect and self-worth.

Self-love involves recognizing our own value and treating ourselves with kindness, compassion, and respect. It means accepting ourselves for who we are, flaws and all, and understanding that our worth is not determined by external factors such as achievements or appearances.

When we love ourselves, we are better equipped to set healthy boundaries, which is essential for healthy relationships. We are better able to communicate our needs and expectations and to say no when necessary. This not only protects us from harm but also allows us to show up fully in our relationships with others.

Self-love also involves taking care of ourselves physically, emotionally, and spiritually. This means getting enough sleep, eating well, exercising, and engaging in activities that bring us joy and fulfillment. It means seeking out support when we need it and prioritizing our own well-being.

However, self-love is not always easy. Many of us struggle with negative self-talk, self-doubt, and self-criticism. We may have internalized messages from our past that tell us we are not good enough or that we do not deserve love. Overcoming these beliefs and cultivating self-love can be a lifelong journey, but it is one that is essential for a fulfilling and meaningful life.

Practicing self-love involves several steps. The first step is to become aware of our thoughts and beliefs about ourselves. We must recognize when we are engaging in negative self-talk or self-criticism and challenge these beliefs. This can involve reframing negative thoughts into positive ones or seeking support from a therapist or coach.

The second step is to prioritize our own needs and well-being. This means taking time for self-care and setting boundaries that honor our needs and values. It also means recognizing when we need help and seeking support from friends, family, or professionals.

The third step is to cultivate self-compassion. This involves treating ourselves with the same kindness and understanding that we would extend to a friend who is struggling. It means recognizing that we are human and imperfect and that it is okay to make mistakes or experience setbacks.

When we practice self-love, we create a solid foundation for loving others.

We are better able to extend compassion, kindness, and understanding to others because we have experienced it ourselves. We are also better equipped to set healthy boundaries and communicate our needs in relationships, which allows us to show up fully and authentically in our connections with others.

In conclusion, self-love is not selfish or egotistical, but rather an essential component of loving others. When we love ourselves, we create a solid foundation for healthy relationships and are better equipped to extend love to others. Cultivating self-love involves becoming aware of our thoughts and beliefs, prioritizing our own needs and well-being, and practicing self-compassion. By doing so, we can create a more loving and compassionate world, starting with ourselves.

7

Loving Your Neighbors: Reaching Out to Those Around You

The beauty of connecting with others.

In the previous chapters, we have discussed the importance of love and the challenges that come with extending love to others. We have also explored the importance of loving ourselves as the foundation for loving others. In this chapter, we will focus on loving our neighbors and reaching out to those around us.

Loving our neighbors means extending love and compassion to those in our immediate community, whether they are friends, family, or strangers. It means recognizing the humanity in others and treating them with kindness and respect. It involves reaching out to those who are struggling or in need and extending a helping hand.

Many of us live in communities where we do not know our neighbors or feel disconnected from those around us. We may be hesitant to reach out to others for fear of rejection or judgment. However, reaching out to our neighbors is an essential component of creating a more loving and connected world.

There are many ways to reach out to our neighbors and extend love and compassion. We can start by simply saying hello or introducing ourselves to those we see on a regular basis. We can offer to help with tasks or errands, such as picking up groceries or walking a dog. We can organize community events or participate in neighborhood groups or associations.

We can also reach out to those who may be struggling or in need, such as the elderly or those experiencing financial hardship. We can offer to provide meals or assistance with chores or errands. We can volunteer at local charities or organizations that serve those in need.

Reaching out to our neighbors can also involve extending love and compassion to those who are different from us. This may include individuals from different cultural, religious, or socio-economic backgrounds. By recognizing and celebrating our differences, we can create a more inclusive and loving community.

However, reaching out to our neighbors is not always easy. We may encounter resistance or rejection, or we may be unsure of how to help. It is important to approach these situations with empathy and understanding and to recognize that everyone has their own unique struggles and challenges.

Loving our neighbors also involves setting healthy boundaries and taking care of our own well-being. We must recognize when we are taking on too much or neglecting our own needs, and we must be willing to say no when necessary. This allows us to show up fully and authentically in our relationships with others.

In conclusion, loving our neighbors is an essential component of creating a more loving and connected world. It involves reaching out to those around us, extending kindness and compassion, and recognizing and celebrating our differences. Reaching out to our neighbors can be challenging, but it is important to approach these situations with empathy and understanding. By loving our neighbors, we create a more inclusive and compassionate world for all.

8

Loving Your Enemies: The Ultimate Test of Love

It is hard to do, but worth it.

One of the most challenging aspects of love is extending it to those who have hurt us or whom we consider our enemies. It goes against our natural instincts to love those who have caused us pain or harm. However, as followers of God, we are called to extend love and forgiveness even to our enemies.

Loving our enemies does not mean condoning their behavior or allowing them to continue to harm us. It means recognizing their humanity and extending kindness and compassion despite the hurt they have caused us. It involves breaking the cycle of hate and revenge and choosing to respond with love instead.

In Matthew 5:44, Jesus said, "But I tell you, love your enemies and pray for those who persecute you." This is a radical and challenging call to action, but it is essential for those who wish to follow in the footsteps of Jesus.

Loving our enemies can take many forms. It may involve reaching out to them and attempting to reconcile and rebuild a relationship. It may involve forgiving them and letting go of anger and resentment. It may also involve praying for them and extending kindness and compassion from a distance.

Loving our enemies can be a difficult and painful process, but it is ultimately freeing and transformative. It allows us to let go of bitterness and resentment and to move towards healing and wholeness. It also allows us to model the love and compassion of God to those around us.

However, loving our enemies is not always easy. We may struggle with feelings of anger, hurt, and betrayal. We may be hesitant to extend forgiveness or reach out to those who have hurt us. It is important to recognize these feelings and to seek support and guidance from trusted friends or spiritual mentors.

It is also important to remember that loving our enemies does not mean allowing them to continue to harm us. We must set healthy boundaries and protect ourselves from further harm. This may involve seeking outside help or removing ourselves from the situation.

In addition to extending love to our enemies, we must also strive to understand and address the root causes of their behavior. This may involve addressing issues of injustice, poverty, or inequality. It may also involve seeking to understand the perspectives and experiences of those who have hurt us.

Loving our enemies is the ultimate test of love. It requires us to break down barriers and extend love and compassion even to those who have caused us pain. It is a radical and transformative call to action, but it is essential for those who wish to follow in the footsteps of Jesus. By loving our enemies, we model the love and compassion of God and contribute to a more just and peaceful world.

9

The Rewards of Loving: Finding Joy, Peach, and Purpose

Loving produces exponential returns.

Loving others is not always easy. It requires us to put ourselves aside and extend ourselves towards others, often at great personal cost. However, the rewards of loving are many and significant, not only for those we love but also for ourselves.

One of the primary rewards of loving is joy. When we extend love and compassion to others, we experience a sense of joy and fulfillment that comes from knowing that we have made a positive impact in someone else's life. Joy is a byproduct of love, and it is something that cannot be achieved through material possessions or external success.

Loving others also brings us a sense of peace. When we choose to love instead of hate, we break down barriers and promote understanding and unity. This can lead to a sense of peace and harmony within ourselves and in our relationships with others. Peace is something that is often elusive in our fast-paced and chaotic world, but it is something that can be found through the practice of love.

Another reward of loving is purpose. When we extend love and compassion towards others, we are fulfilling a fundamental purpose of our existence, which is to love and be loved. Loving others gives us a sense of purpose and meaning in our lives, as we are contributing to the well-being of others and the world around us.

Furthermore, loving others can have a positive impact on our own mental and physical health. Studies have shown that people who practice love and compassion towards others experience reduced stress and anxiety, improved mood, and better overall physical health. When we love others, we are not only benefiting them, but we are also benefiting ourselves.

Finally, the rewards of loving extend beyond our immediate relationships and into the world at large. When we extend love and compassion towards others, we are contributing to a more just, peaceful, and loving world. Our actions can have a ripple effect, inspiring others to practice love and compassion towards others as well. In this way, the rewards of loving extend far beyond ourselves and into the world around us.

In conclusion, the rewards of loving are many and significant. Joy, peace, purpose, improved health, and a more just and peaceful world are just some of the rewards that come from practicing love and compassion towards others. While loving others can be challenging at times, it is ultimately a rewarding and fulfilling way to live our lives. As we extend love and compassion towards others, we not only benefit them but also ourselves and the world around us.

10

Love in Action: Making a Difference in Your Community

People need you.

Loving others is not just about feeling warm and fuzzy inside; it is about taking action to improve the lives of those around us. One of the most powerful ways to put love into action is by making a difference in our communities. Whether we live in a small town or a big city, there are always opportunities to make a positive impact in the lives of others.

One way to make a difference is by volunteering our time and talents to organizations that serve our community. Whether it's a local food bank, a homeless shelter, or a youth center, there are countless organizations that rely on volunteers to provide critical services to those in need. Volunteering not only benefits the organization and those they serve, but it also benefits us as volunteers by allowing us to connect with others and find meaning and purpose in our lives.

Another way to make a difference is by using our resources to support causes that we care about. This can be as simple as donating money to a local charity or as complex as starting our own non-profit organization. By using our resources to support causes that we believe in, we can make a tangible impact in the lives of others and contribute to a better world.

We can also make a difference in our communities by advocating for change. This can involve attending city council meetings, writing letters to elected officials, or participating in peaceful protests. By using our voices to advocate for change, we can help to create a more just and equitable society for all.

In addition to these actions, we can also make a difference in our communities by simply being kind and compassionate towards those around us. This can involve reaching out to a neighbor in need, volunteering to mow an elderly person's lawn, or simply smiling at a stranger. Small acts of kindness can have a significant impact on those around us, and they can create a ripple effect of love and compassion in our communities.

Ultimately, making a difference in our communities requires us to take action and put love into practice. It requires us to be intentional and proactive in our efforts to improve the lives of those around us. By doing so, we can create a more just, loving, and compassionate world for all.

In conclusion, loving our communities is an essential aspect of living a life of love. By volunteering our time and talents, supporting causes that we care about, advocating for change, and being kind and compassionate towards those around us, we can make a positive impact in the lives of others and create a more just and equitable society.

Loving our communities requires us to take action and put love into practice, but the rewards of doing so are immeasurable. As we extend love and compassion towards our communities, we are not only making a difference in the lives of others, but we are also contributing to a better world for all.

11

Love in Dark Times: How to Find Hope and Comfort

Desire and wish for love.

Life can be difficult and challenging, and there are times when it can be hard to find hope and comfort. It is during these dark times that we need love the most. Love can provide us with the strength and resilience that we need to overcome adversity, and it can help us to find hope and comfort even in the darkest of times.

One of the most important things to remember during dark times is that we are not alone. We all go through struggles and challenges, and it is important to reach out to others for support and comfort. This can involve talking to a friend or family member, seeking the help of a therapist or counselor, or finding comfort in a spiritual community. By connecting with others, we can find the love and support that we need to navigate difficult times.

Another way to find hope and comfort during dark times is by engaging in self-care practices that nurture our physical, mental, and emotional well-being. This can involve taking time for ourselves, engaging in activities that we enjoy, getting enough rest and exercise, and nourishing our bodies with healthy foods. By taking care of ourselves, we can build resilience and cultivate a sense of inner peace and well-being.

We can also find hope and comfort by practicing gratitude and focusing on the positive aspects of our lives. Even in the darkest of times, there is always something to be grateful for, whether it's a loving friend or family member, a beautiful sunset, or the opportunity to make a difference in the world. By focusing on the positive, we can shift our perspective and find hope and comfort even in the midst of adversity.

Another important aspect of finding hope and comfort during dark times is by cultivating a spiritual practice. This can involve meditation, prayer, or other practices that connect us to something greater than ourselves. By cultivating a sense of connection to the divine, we can find a sense of peace and comfort that transcends our current circumstances.

Ultimately, finding hope and comfort during dark times requires us to cultivate a sense of love and compassion towards others and ourselves. By extending love and compassion towards ourselves, we can build resilience and cultivate inner peace and well-being. By extending love and compassion towards others, we can build connection and find comfort in the knowledge that we are not alone in our struggles.

In conclusion, love is essential to finding hope and comfort during dark times. By connecting with others, engaging in self-care practices, practicing gratitude, cultivating a spiritual practice, and extending love and compassion towards ourselves and others, we can find the strength and resilience that we need to navigate difficult times. While life can be challenging and difficult, we can find hope and comfort by embracing the power of love and cultivating a sense of connection and compassion towards others and ourselves.

12

The Legacy of Love: Leaving a Lasting Impact on the World

A little love can make lifetime changes.

Love has the power to change the world. It can inspire us to great acts of kindness and compassion, and it can bring hope and healing to those who are hurting. When we choose to live a life of love, we have the opportunity to leave a lasting impact on the world around us.

One of the key ways to leave a legacy of love is by cultivating meaningful relationships with others. This can involve nurturing our friendships and family connections, as well as seeking out opportunities to connect with those in our community who may be in need of love and support. By building these relationships, we can create a network of love and compassion that can extend far beyond our own lives.

Another important way to leave a legacy of love is by serving others. This can involve volunteering our time and resources to organizations and causes that we care about, as well as seeking out opportunities to make a positive impact in our daily lives. By serving others, we can make a tangible difference in the world around us and leave a lasting legacy of love and compassion.

We can also leave a legacy of love by living a life of integrity and authenticity. This involves being true to ourselves and living in alignment with our values and beliefs. When we live in this way, we inspire others to do the same, and we create a ripple effect of love and positivity that can extend far beyond our own lives.

Another important aspect of leaving a legacy of love is by cultivating a sense of gratitude and generosity. When we are grateful for what we have and generous with our resources, we create a culture of abundance and kindness that can impact the world in profound ways. By living a life of generosity and gratitude, we can inspire others to do the same and create a legacy of love and abundance that will continue to flourish long after we are gone.

Ultimately, leaving a legacy of love requires us to be intentional about the way we live our lives. It involves making a conscious choice to live a life of love, compassion, and generosity, and to create a ripple effect of positivity that can extend far beyond our own lives. When we choose to live in this way, we can make a lasting impact on the world around us and leave a legacy of love that will continue to inspire and uplift for generations to come.

In conclusion, the legacy of love is a powerful and inspiring concept. By cultivating meaningful relationships, serving others, living a life of integrity and authenticity, and cultivating a sense of gratitude and generosity, we can leave a lasting impact on the world around us. While it may not always be easy to live a life of love and compassion, it is always worth it. By choosing to live in this way, we can make a positive difference in the world and leave a legacy of love that will continue to inspire and uplift for generations to come.

13

John Emerges from a Como and Begins to Love

Everyone is capable of loving.

On day four, discussions on pulling the plug were ongoing. After extensive treatment and care from medical professionals, John finally emerged from his coma. It was a slow process, but eventually, he started to show signs of consciousness. At first, he could only open his eyes and make simple movements. But as time went on, he began to communicate with those around him.

It was a joyous moment for John's family and friends when he started to recognize them and speak to them. When he woke up, he was in a lot of pain. He had lost a lot of weight and muscle strength during his time in a coma, but with the help of physical therapy, he was able to regain his strength and start moving around again. John had to stay in the hospital for several more weeks. He had to undergo physical therapy to regain his strength.

The road to recovery was not easy, but John was determined to get back to his normal life. He worked hard with his doctors and therapists, and eventually, he was able to return to flying planes. It was a huge accomplishment for John and a testament to his perseverance and resilience.

John recalled that supernatural spiritual encounter he had with a voice that he recognized as the voice of God. The voice said, "Your job is to love!"

John was stunned. He had never heard anything like this before, and he couldn't believe that God was speaking directly to him. "Your job is to love," the voice said. He was startled. He didn't know where the voice came from, but it was clear and strong.

Shell shocked from the emergence from a coma and the voice he had heard.

"What do you mean, God?" John asked.
"Your job is to love," the memory repeated.

John had an awakening and realized he had received a second chance on life.

John knew that he had a lot of work to do in order to fulfill his new mission. He had to learn how to love others in a deeper and more meaningful way, and he had to let go of some of the selfish desires that had driven him in the past.

"Love your family and friends. Love your neighbors. Love your enemies. Love everyone, unconditionally."

"It's not always easy," God's voice said. "But it's possible. And it's the most important thing you can do."

John sat in silence for hours, trying to process what he had heard from God.

"But how?" John asked. "How can I love everyone?"

John thought about what the voice had said for a long time. And then, John decided to try. He decided to love everyone, unconditionally.

It wasn't easy. There were times when John wanted to give up. But he kept trying. And slowly, but surely, he began to see a difference.

John started to feel more connected to the people around me. He started to feel more at peace with himself. And he started to feel more like he was living a purposeful life.

John is still not perfect. He still makes mistakes. But he is trying his best to love everyone, unconditionally. And he knows that it's the most important thing he can do.

If you're feeling lost and confused, John's encourages you to pray and ask God for guidance. Ask Him to show you what He wants you to do with your life. And then, listen for His voice. It may not be as clear as John's voice was, but it will be there.

And remember, your job is to love.

Over time, John began to put his new mission into action. He started volunteering at a local hospital, spending time with patients and listening to their stories. He also began reaching out to friends and family members, showing them more love and support than ever before.

As he did these things, John found that his life was filled with a newfound sense of purpose and meaning. He no longer felt lost or aimless, but instead felt like he was making a real difference in the world.

Looking back on his life, John realized that hearing God's message had been the turning point that he had been searching for. Without that experience, he might have continued on his old path, never realizing the true meaning of his life.

But now, with a renewed sense of purpose and a deep commitment to love others, John knew that he was exactly where he was meant to be. And he was grateful to have heard God's message when he did, as it had changed his life in the most profound way imaginable.

It took John a long time to recover from necrotizing fasciitis. But he eventually made a fantastic recovery. He is able to walk and has even obtained a Federal Aviation Administration (FAA) special issuance medical certificate. John is flying again and is very thankful to be back in the skies.

John's ailment is a reminder that necrotizing fasciitis is a serious disease. If you think you might have necrotizing fasciitis, it is important to see a doctor right away. Early diagnosis and treatment are essential for a good outcome. John's long hard work to recovery provides lessons of hope and inspiration. Even in the face of adversity, he never gave up and was able to overcome the challenges that lay before him.

John's story is a reminder to love. John now has an overwhelming sense of love and acceptance, and a deeper appreciation for the beauty of life and its fragility. He has a newfound understanding of his purpose and place in the world, and a newfound respect for the interconnectedness of all things. He has a newfound understanding of the power of love and has even greater capacity for love, both for himself and for others. He has an increase sense of empathy, compassion, and understanding, and a greater openness to giving and receiving love. John took advantage of his second chance of life to love more and to increase his capacity to give and receive love.

14

John's Story: A Source of Love and Inspiration

The spread of love from God's voice.

John's story has profoundly impacted my life, igniting a passion for philanthropy within me. As a philanthropist, I dedicate my time, money, and resources to assist those in need through charitable acts. The act of helping others not only brings me immense joy but also allows me to contribute positively to both humanity and the planet. The act of giving grants me a sense of renewal, instills gratitude within me, and fosters inner peace. Moreover, giving enhances my self-esteem and provides a profound sense of belonging. It is through acts of giving that lives can be saved, as a simple meal for a starving individual can make a significant difference. Volunteering has proven to enhance stress management skills, reduce rates of depression, alleviate loneliness, and increase overall life satisfaction. Undoubtedly, these factors significantly contribute to our long-term health and well-being.

In my commitment to philanthropy, I actively donate to various charity relief services. One such organization is a humanitarian charity that began its mission in 1943. Devoted to aiding the world's impoverished, this charity has earned a four-star rating. Impressively, 93 percent of their total expenses are allocated directly to the programs and services they offer.

Additionally, I contribute to another long-standing charitable organization, dedicated to combating poverty in America. With a history spanning over 75 years, this organization stands as the fifth-largest charity in the United States. It too boasts a four-star rating, with 93 percent of its total expenses dedicated to program delivery. Operating through local chapters across the nation, this organization's impact is felt throughout communities.

Recognizing the significance of supporting one's local community, I encourage others to donate to their nearby church, synagogue, mosque, or community organizations. Charitable institutions of all kinds rely on financial support, particularly during the holiday season, where many churches hold giving services in desperate need of contributions.

For those who find themselves with limited financial means, time can be just as valuable. I actively participate in the social ministries of my church, particularly in providing meals to the hungry. By engaging in this service, we procure food, prepare meals, and serve them to those in dire need. A typical meal consists of a hearty ham and potato gratin casserole, complemented by salad, beans, fruit, rolls, desserts, iced tea, milk, and water. Furthermore, I assist in delivering meals for the Foodbank, ensuring that those facing hunger receive the sustenance they require. Witnessing the gratitude expressed by someone who looks me in the eye and sincerely says thank you as they receive a meal is profoundly rewarding. The exchange of love in these moments is truly remarkable.

Another individual with a generous spirit and I oversee six garden vegetable plots within our church community. Together, we cultivate, plant, weed, water, and harvest various vegetables. Every last Saturday of the month, our church donates this fresh produce, along with toiletries and clothing, to those in need. By incorporating the harvest from our vegetable garden into the church's food pantry, we contribute to the monthly distribution, ensuring that nutritious food reaches those who require it most.

Moreover, I have been fortunate enough to collaborate with six other adults and eight teen leaders to teach religion to teenagers. It is often ironic how, in the process of teaching, these teenagers impart invaluable lessons and knowledge to me as well.

Recognizing the constant need for blood donations, I regularly contribute double red cell donations several times a year. By giving two units of red blood cells, I aid others in need while also reaping certain health benefits for myself.

Even while traveling, I make it a point to offer assistance to local churches during layovers. Remarkably, I have never been turned down, as there is always some task or project that requires human labor and support.

In a previous book, "Ten Healthy Tips," I aimed to give back to humanity in yet another way. This book delves into the mind of an airline pilot, sharing the health tips he practiced throughout his career. By providing a flight plan for readers to enhance their well-being and improve both mental and physical health, I hoped to make a positive impact. If just one healthy tip could help a single person in any way, I would consider myself richly rewarded, knowing that I have contributed to the betterment of mankind through love and generosity.

I wish to emphasize that I do not share these endeavors to boast or elevate my actions above those of others who have done remarkable things for people. Rather, I present them as a few examples of how I express my love for humanity. By engaging in these acts of kindness, I fulfill what I believe to be a fundamental purpose of our existence: to love and be loved. It is through these efforts that I strive to purify and illuminate my soul, ensuring that on the day I depart from this world, God will not send me to hell—perhaps purgatory, or hopefully, to heaven.

Should this book influence even one person to extend love to another, I would consider myself amply rewarded. Ultimately, my revised lifelong goal of aiding mankind would be realized. The capacity to love knows no age or boundaries. Regardless of our past experiences or current circumstances, we all possess the ability to start loving others today. Every individual has the potential to love.

John revealed to me, "Frank, God appeared to me and said, 'Your job is to love.'"

And always remember, your job is to love.

Bonus

Below is my special prayer I want to share with you. This prayer helps me to love. I want to share this prayer with you hoping it will help you.

At the end of my day before my human body falls asleep, I reflect on my day and say prayers. Usually, the transition from waking to sleeping takes about five to fifteen minutes for my body to settle down. This is an opportune time for reflection and to pray prayers.

When I am dead tired and short on time sometimes, I just pray the "Trinity for Me" prayer to sum up my life that day. What am I thankful for and how can God help me, if He wills it? Who did I not love today and how can God help me better to love that person or persons? God help me to love.

*Thank You for*_____. (Customize to your situation).

*Please help and/or grant me this request*_____. (Customize to your situation).

Customize and fill in the blanks according to your situation. Everyone needs to be thankful. Everyone needs help sometimes.

TRINITY FOR ME

O my dear God
O my dear Jesus
And the Holy Spirit,
Thank You for this moment of life.
Thank You for this breath of air.
Thank You for providing water and
food for my body,
And thank You for protecting,
guiding, and nourishing my soul.
Thank You for
_____.
Please help and/or grant me with
_____.
Please protect and guide my
thoughts, words, heart, and soul
Toward you during this earthly
journey so that after this life I will be
in heaven.
Please help me to love God, myself,
and everyone.
I love you, trust you, believe in you,
and hope to be with you.
Amen.

Acknowledgments

To the over 1,000 pilots I have flown with, who have shaped my pilot personality and influenced the pilot I have become, I thank you for those safe flights and experiences. I thank John for the many walks and laughs we shared, and for opening up his heart and revealing his experience with God's call to him. Thank you Bill Schwartz for your contribution to the front cover background. I thank my loving wife and God for giving me the precious opportunity to be a father. To my sons, who always inspire me, I wish the best of all good things to come to you in this earthly life and the life after.

Website- www.frankjdonohue.com

About The Author

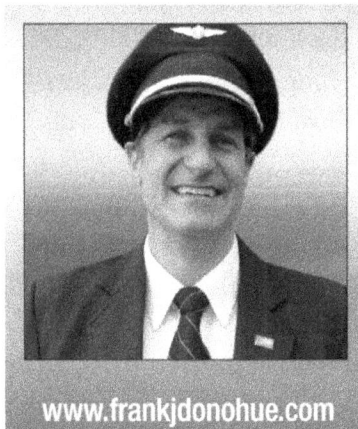

www.frankjdonohue.com

Frank J. Donohue, born in New York, is an American pilot, author, publisher and video producer. He earned his bachelor's degree and several pilot licenses at Embry-Riddle Aeronautical University after serving one tour of duty in the United States Air Force. Frank holds the Airline Transport Pilot license, Flight Instructor license, Advanced and Instrument Ground Instructor licenses, Flight Engineer License, Aircraft Dispatcher license and Remote Pilot Certificate. With over 36 years of flying experience, Frank received a prestigious pilot award for over

30 years of impeccable service for a very distinguished career of flying excellence with FedEx in 2018.

Frank is the author of *School and Schooled*, #1 Bestselling author of *Ten Healthy Tips*, author of *From Hate to Love*, author of #1 Bestselling author *Frank the Pilot*, and author of *God Said to me*. Frank is the owner and creator of NOT-Y a pilot video channel featuring pilot flight and non-flight stories. Frank lives in Virginia Beach with his wife. They have two grown children. He enjoys traveling, gardening, fishing and helping people through various philanthropic organizations.

Author's Note

God Said to Me, "your Job is to Love" was written, designed, produced and published by its author to the same high standards as the mainstream publishing industry. It is really hard to put a good book together. I invite you to post an honest and objective review of this book in the online bookstore of your choice. Your comments will help improve the quality of what good writers write and what good readers read. Thank you for your time and service. You can contact Frank J. Donohue on FB, LinkedIn, TikTok, Twitter and Instagram and visit his websites:www.frankjdonohue.com, and www.not-y.com.

One minute Love videos posted on:

TikTok = **NOT_Y4U**

Instagram = **LOVENOTYY4U**

Meta/FB = **NOT-Y** (thru Frank J Donohue)

YouTube = **NOT-Y** (/@not-y2241)

Thank you for following me.

End of book